knowledge
does not diminish our pain;
it helps us overcome it.

A gift for: _____

From: _____

when we HURT

prayer, preparation, & hope for life's pain

PHILIP YANCEY

inspirio™

contents

Doctor
Paul Brand

was a world-renowned hand surgeon and leprosy specialist. His years of pioneering work among leprosy patients earned him numerous awards and honors, including the prestigious Albert Lasker Award, the Damien-Duton Award, and the Commander of the Order of the British Empire (presented by Queen Elizabeth II). As Chief of Rehabilitation at the leprosy center in Carville, Louisiana, he earned the Distinguished Service Award from the Public Health Service.

Former Surgeon General C. Everett Koop said, "As a surgeon, scholar, investigator, and philosopher gifted with rare insight, Paul Brand has lived and worked among the pain-afflicted. His extraordinary experiences have a strong thematic unity which allows him to present a rather startling perspective on pain. He opens the window onto new ways of looking at pain, and that translates into something of worth. Paul Brand offers an opportunity to look at pain not as your enemy, but as your friend."

Dr. Brand died in 2003 from complications after a fall.

This is his story.

Pain does not occur in the abstract — no sensation is more **personal** or more importunate.

Dr. Paul Brand

My professional life has revolved around the theme of pain, and by living in different cultures, I have observed at close hand diverse attitudes toward it. My life divides roughly into thirds—twenty-seven years in India, twenty-five years in England, and more than thirty years in the United States—and from each society I have learned something new about pain.

Each of these groups of people—Londoners who during the Blitz suffered gladly for a cause, Indians who expected suffering and learned not to fear it, and Americans who suffered less but feared it more—helped to form my outlook on this mysterious fact of human existence. Most of us will one day face severe pain. I am convinced that the attitude we cultivate in advance may well determine how suffering will affect us when it does strike. Out of that conviction comes this book.

Few experiences in life are more universal than pain, which flows like lava beneath the crust of daily life. For good and for ill, the human species has among its privileges the preeminence of pain. We have the unique ability to step outside ourselves and self-reflect, by reading a book about pain, for example, or by summoning up the memory of a terrifying ordeal. Some pains—the pain of grief or emotional trauma—have no physical stimulus whatever. They are states of mind, concocted by the alchemy of the brain. These feats of consciousness make it possible for suffering to loiter in the mind long after the body's need for it has passed. Yet they also give us the potential to attain an outlook that will change the very landscape of the pain experience. We can learn to cope, and even to triumph.

When pain is to be borne, a little courage helps more than much knowledge, a little human sympathy more than much courage, and the least tincture of the love of God more than all.

C.S. Lewis

Be courageous. Offer your pains to God. Pray for the strength to endure. Above all, develop a habit of conversing often with God. Adore him in your infirmities. At the very height of your suffering, ask him humbly and affectionately (as a child to a good parent) to help you to accept his will.

Brother Lawrence

an appreciation for pain

If I were to choose between pain and nothing, I would choose **pain**.

William Faulkner

In India we had determined that almost all the deformities in leprosy came about because the disease destroyed the ability to sense pain. People with leprosy damaged themselves because they lacked pain's warning system.

In November 1972, about the same time I was reconciling myself to the failure of a project to detect pain, I received word that my daughter Mary had delivered our first grandson. Some months passed before I could make my way to Minnesota to investigate this new phenomenon. When I arrived, Mary proudly presented a healthy boy named Daniel. I confess that for a few minutes I slipped back into my orthopedist's role, examining his finger joints, the curve in his spine, the angle of his feet, all of which checked out splendidly. There was one more test to conduct, however, and I waited until Mary left the room before trying it.

With an ordinary
straight pin, I performed a
simple evaluation of the pain system
on the tip of one finger. I was gentle, of course,
but I had to do it. Daniel yanked his hand back,
frowned, looked at the finger, and then looked at
me. He was normal! His reflex worked according
to design, and already at his young age he was
learning an important lesson about straight pins.
I held him close to my chest and prayed a prayer
of thanksgiving for that tiny finger. The most
elaborate glove we had developed at Carville
included a grand total of twenty transducers and
cost us nearly ten thousand dollars. This toddler
came equipped with a thousand pain detectors
in that one fingertip alone, each calibrated to a
threshold specific to the fingertip. I felt a little
grandfatherly pride, because my own

personal genetic code was involved in the making of that little boy. As an engineer I had failed to create a pain system with my expensive electronic transducers, but my DNA had wildly succeeded.

It defied my comprehension that Daniel's miniature transducers would be able to sift through the many varieties of traumatic, constant, and repetitive stress and report into the spinal column, with no short-circuits in the wiring and no need for outside maintenance, for a period of seventy or eighty years. More, these pain sensors would work whether he wanted them to or not; the switch was out of reach. The sensors were accurate, they were prompts, and they compelled a response, even from a brain too young to comprehend the meaning of danger. I ended my prayer with a familiar refrain, "Thank God for pain!"

God created
man
   in his own image,
   in the image of God he created him;
   male and female he created them...
God saw all that he had made, and it was
   very good.

Genesis 1:27,31

Everything God created is good, and
nothing is to be rejected if it is received with
thanksgiving.

1 Timothy 4:4

For you created my inmost being;
   you knit me together in my mother's womb.
I praise you because I am fearfully and
     wonderfully made;
   your works are wonderful,
   I know that full well.

Psalm 139:13–14

I first learned about painlessness while working with leprosy, a disease that afflicts more than 12 million people worldwide. Leprosy has long provoked a fear bordering on hysteria, mainly because of the horrible disfigurement that may result if it goes untreated. But my most difficult patients were those with the rare condition that made them totally insensitive to pain. More than a hundred cases of congenital painlessness have been written up in medical literature. For the painless, danger lurks everywhere. A larynx that never feels a tickle does not trigger the cough reflex that relocates phlegm from the lungs to the pharynx, and a person who never coughs runs the risk of developing pneumonia. The bone joints of insensitive people deteriorate because there are not whispers of pain encouraging a shift in position, and soon bone grinds against bone.

Strep throat, appendicitis, heart attack, stroke—the body has no way to announce these threats to the painless person.

Pain is not the enemy, but the loyal scout announcing the enemy. And yet—here is the central paradox of my life—after spending a lifetime among people who destroy themselves for lack of pain, I still find it difficult to communicate an appreciation for pain to people who have no such defect. Pain truly is the gift nobody wants. I can think of nothing more precious for those who suffer from congenital painlessness, leprosy, diabetes, and other disorders. But people who already own this gift rarely value it. Usually, they resent it.

In the modern view, pain is an enemy, a sinister invader that must be expelled. And if Product X removes pain thirty seconds faster, all the better. This approach has a crucial, dangerous flaw: once regarded as an enemy, not a warning signal, pain loses its power to instruct.

I long for a commercial that at least acknowledges some benefit to pain: "First, listen to your pain. It is your own body talking to you." I, too, may take an aspirin to relieve a tension headache, but only after pausing to ask what brought on the nervous tension that provoked the headache. I have taken antacid for stomach pain, but not before considering what I might have eaten to give me such pain. Did I eat too much? Too fast? Pain is no invading enemy, but a loyal messenger dispatched by my own body to alert me to some danger.

I thank you, Lord, for pain.
For most of every day, Father,
I live in total unawareness of thy gift of pain,
which only whispers its advice.
And when with thoughtless zeal I move in
    danger zones,
or when a wounded limb needs rest so it
    can heal,
then pain in sharp crescendo screams
    an agonizing plea
that dominates all action and all thought.
Give me grace, O Lord, not only to obey
    the shrill command
but even to be thankful for the hurt that
    keeps me whole,
for the fetters which allow me to be free.

Dr. Paul Brand

living well with pain

Pain is a
priceless
essential gift—of that I have no doubt.
And yet only by learning to master pain
can we keep it from mastering us.

Dr. Paul Brand

It was while treating leprosy patients in India that I first recognized the value of the gift of pain, and afterward I tried to convey that sense to my six children. *Is it possible to teach appreciation for pain to a child?* I wondered. After a few bungled attempts, I concluded that a five-year-old child screaming in panic at the sight of his own blood is not receptive to such a message. My children seemed much more open to an object lesson when *I* was the victim of cuts and scrapes.

"Does it hurt, Daddy?" the children would ask as I rinsed out a cut on my hand and scrubbed it with soap. I would explain that yes, it hurt, but that was a good thing. The tenderness would make me take extra care. I would skip my weeding chores in the garden for a few days in order to give my injured hand a rest. Pain, I pointed out, gave me a great advantage over our friends Namo, Sadan, and the other leprosy patients. My wound would likely heal faster, with less danger of complications, because I felt pain.

Pain is part of
the body's **magic**.
It is the way the body
transmits a sign to the brain that
something is wrong.

Norman Cousins

Every good and perfect gift is from
above, coming down from the Father
of the heavenly lights.

James 1:17

the three stages of pain

I am not a "pain expert" in the traditional sense. I have never worked in a pain clinic and have had limited experience in pain management. Instead, I came to appreciate the subtleties of pain by treating those who do not feel it. I certainly never said, "Thank God for pain!" as a child in the Kolli hills of India or in medical school during the Blitz in London; that outlook came after years of working among victims of painlessness.

Over the years, I have tried to fit together an approach that includes what I learned from the painless, as well as from those of us who feel pain. We cannot live well without pain, but how do we best live with it?

I divide the experience of pain into three stages. First, there is the pain *signal*, an alarm that goes off when nerve endings in the periphery sense danger. My ill-fated project to develop "a practical substitute for pain" was an attempt to reproduce pain at this first, most basic level.

At a second stage of pain, the spinal cord and base of the brain act as a "spinal gate" to sort out which of the many millions of signals deserve to be forwarded as a *message* to the brain. Damage or disease may sometimes interfere: if the spinal cord is severed, as in paraplegia, peripheral nerve endings below the break may continue to discharge pain signals, but those signals will not reach the brain.

The final stage of pain takes place in the higher brain (especially the cerebral cortex), which sorts through the prescreened messages and decides on a *response.* Indeed, pain does not truly exist until the entire cycle of signal, message, and response has been completed.

A simple, everyday mishap—a little girl's fall while running—illustrates the interplay among these three stages of pain. When her knee first scrapes against the sidewalk, she rolls sideways to avoid further contact. This emergency maneuver, ordered by the spinal cord, takes place at the reflex level (stage one). Half a second passes before the girl becomes conscious of stinging sensations from her scraped knee. How she then responds will depend on the severity of the scrape, her own personality makeup, and what else is going on around her.

If the girl is running in a race with friends, chances are the noise and overall excitement of play will produce competing messages (stage two) that block the further progress of the pain. She may get up and finish the race without even glancing at her knee. When the race is over, though, and the excitement dies down, pain messages will likely stream through the spinal gate to the thinking part of the brain (stage three). The girl looks at the knee, sees blood, and now the conscious brain takes over. Fear enhances the pain. Mother becomes important, and that is where the child turns. A wise mother first hugs her daughter, replacing the fear with reassurance. Then she fusses over the sore, washes away the blood, covers the wound with a decorative adhesive bandage, and sends the child back to play. The girl forgets about the pain.

All this time the actual pain signals have not changed much. Loyal neurons in the knee have been sending in damage reports all afternoon and evening. The girl's perception of the pain varies mostly by the extent to which the pain was blocked at stage two, by competing input, and at stage three, by the parent's resourcefulness in calming anxiety.

In adults, who have a larger pool of experience and emotions to draw from, the mind plays a more paramount role. As a doctor I have gained an ever-increasing appreciation for the mind's ability to alter the perception of pain in one direction or the other. We can become adept at converting pain into the more serious state that we call *suffering*. Or, to the contrary, we can learn to harness the vast resource of the conscious mind to help cope with the pain.

I would like to be spared pain, dear God.
It comes after me anyway.
Sometimes it's physical pain.
Often it's emotional.
Occasionally it may be intellectual or
   spiritual.
Let me know that I am never away from
   your love,
no matter how miserable my
      circumstances.

Bernard Bangley

In medical school I mainly encountered pain at stage one. Patients came to me with specific complaints about signals in the periphery. ("My finger hurts." "My stomach aches." "My ears are ringing.") No patient ever said to me something along this line: "Among the many transmissions entering my spinal cord, signals of pain from my finger have been judged of significant value to be forwarded on to the brain." Or, "I am feeling pain in my stomach; could you please administer a morphine-like drug to my brain so that it will ignore the pain signals emanating from my stomach?"

Although I had to rely on the patient's report of stage one to help me diagnose the cause of pain, I soon realized the importance of responding to stage three from the start. Now I would probably rank the stages of pain in the reverse order, giving prominence to the

third stage first.
What takes place in
a person's mind is the most
important aspect of pain—and the
most difficult to treat or even comprehend.
If we can learn to handle pain at this third stage,
we will most likely succeed in keeping pain in its
proper place, as servant and not master.

I first became aware of the power of the mind
when I treated a soldier named Jake, a war hero
who had ignored the pain of shattered legs on
the battlefield, yet who shrank in fear from a
hypodermic needle full of penicillin. Later I
learned that Jake's attitude at the front, strange
as it seemed at the time, was a classic response
to combat injury. Dr. Henry K. Beecher of the
Harvard Medical School coined the term "Anzio
effect" to describe what he observed among
215 casualties from the Anzio beachhead in

World War II. Only one in four soldiers with serious injuries (fractures, amputations, penetrated chests or cerebrums) asked for morphine, though it was freely available. They simply did not need help with the pain, and indeed many of them denied feeling pain at all.

Beecher, an anesthesiologist, contrasted the soldiers' reactions to what he had seen in private practice, where 80 percent of patients recovering from surgical wounds begged for morphine or other narcotics. He concluded, "There is no simple direct relationship between the wound *per se* and the pain experienced. The pain is in very large part determined by other factors, and of great importance here is the significance of the wound…. In the wounded soldier the response to injury was relief, thankfulness at his escape alive from the battlefield, even euphoria; to the civilian, his major surgery was a depressing, calamitous event."

The mind plays an important role in pain because the structure of the brain requires it. Only one-tenth of 1 percent of the fibers entering the cerebral cortex convey new sensory information, including pain messages; all the other nerve cells communicate one with another, reflecting, sifting through memory and emotion. *Am I afraid? Is the pain producing something of value? Do I really want to recover? Am I getting sympathy?*

Pain has no "outside" existence. Two people can look at the same tree; no one has ever shared a stomachache. This is what makes the treatment of pain so difficult. None of us— doctor, parent, or friend—can truly enter into another person's pain. It is the loneliest, most private sensation.

O God, you are my God,
    earnestly I seek you....
On my bed I remember you;
    I think of you through the watches
        of the night.
Because you are my help,
    I sing in the shadow of your wings.
My soul clings to you;
    your right hand upholds me.

Psalm 63:1, 6–8

The

greatest discovery

of my generation is that human beings,
by changing the inner attitudes of their
minds, can change the outer aspects of
their lives.

William James

If I asked my grown children today to recall their most vivid lesson about pain, probably they would all mention the same scene from India. Each summer our entire family piled into a car and drove 280 miles to a magnificent site high in the Nilgiri Hills, an area of virgin jungle still patrolled by tigers and panthers. Our summer bungalow, lent to us by the manager of a tea estate whose staff we had treated as patients, sat in a clearing amid mountain lakes and grasslands some thirty miles from the nearest town. The Webbs often shared our summer bungalow, and it was John Webb, a pediatrician, who prompted the memorable lesson about pain.

Riding his motorcycle on the curvy, unpaved mountain road one day, John had to swerve so sharply to avoid a dog that his wheel caught a rock and flew out from under him.

He fell clear
of the motorcycle,
but momentum sent him
skidding chin-first along the
gravelly path. Although his wounds were
no more serious than scrapes and bruises, tiny
pieces of dirt and gravel had ground into the
flesh.

Knowing my views on pain, John was happy
to let me use him as an object lesson for the
children. "Paul, you know what you have to
do," John said. "And I don't mind if the children
watch." He lay down on the couch, the children
encircling him, and I fetched a basin, plain soap,
and a stiff nail brush. I had no anesthetics to
offer.

During World War II, John had served as a
medical officer in the army that invaded Italy.
He had drilled medics about the importance of
getting every speck of dirt and grime out

of wounds in order to prevent infection. Now that it was his turn, he gritted his teeth and grimaced. I scrubbed the raw flesh with my frothy brush, and our children furnished the sound effects. "Ooh! Yuk!" "I can't watch." "Doesn't it *hurt?*"

"Go on, Paul, go on," John said through clenched teeth if he sensed I was letting up. I scrubbed until I saw nothing but clean pink skin and deeper bleeding dermis, and then applied a soothing antiseptic ointment.

Over the next few days, the children got a short course in physiology as John and I expounded on the magic of blood and skin and their remarkable agents of repair. He took no aspirin or other painkiller, and my children learned that pain can be borne. Perhaps more important, they saw John accepting pain as a valuable part of the recovery process.

Pain was not
given thee merely
to be miserable under;
learn from it, turn it to account.

Thomas Carlyle

Pain is no evil unless it conquer us.

Charles Kingsley

Pain is life—the sharper, the more
evidence of life.

Charles Lamb

My work with pain-deprived patients has proved to me that pain protects us from destroying ourselves. Yet I also know that pain itself can destroy, as any visit to a chronic pain center will show. Unchecked pain saps physical strength and mental energy, and can come to dominate a person's entire life. Somewhere between the two extremes, painlessness and incessant chronic pain, most of us live out our days.

I like the concept of "pain insurance": we can pay up premiums ahead of time, long before pain strikes. The worst time to think about pain, in fact, is when you are feeling its assault, because pain demolishes objectivity. I have made most of my own preparations for pain while healthy, and the insights I gained helped prepare me for later ambushes.

The response to pain is in large degree learned. Ancient Sparta trained its children to prepare for pain. Modern society may have gone to the other extreme; our skill at silencing pain has brought about a kind of cultural atrophy in our overall ability to cope with it. I find some encouraging signs in the younger generation's fondness for aerobics and triathlon competitions, and in the emergence of programs such as Outward Bound. An active body, one that seeks challenges and pushes the limits of endurance, is best equipped to handle unexpected pain when it does occur—and to prepare for it in advance. What often happens, though, is that people who willingly undergo pain for some desirable end find involuntary pain shocking and unmanageable. Pain from illness or injury seems an intrusion in a culture that gives the illusion that all discomfort can be controlled.

Do not conform any longer to the pattern of this world, but be transformed by the renewing of your mind. Then you will be able to test and approve what God's will is—his good, pleasing and perfect will.

Romans 12:2

Those who do not feel pain seldom **think** that it is felt.

Samuel Johnson

gratitude

is the single response most
nourishing to health.

Dr. Hans Selye

Dr. Hans Selye was the true pioneer in
discovering the impact of emotions on health,
and, partly because of his influence, I begin
with gratitude as my first suggestion in
making preparations for pain. Selye found
that such factors as anxiety and depression
can trigger attacks of pain or intensify pain
already present. As Selye summarized his
research toward the end of his life, he named
vengeance and bitterness as the emotional
responses most likely to produce high stress
levels in human beings. Conversely, he
concluded, *gratitude* is the single response
most nourishing to health. I find myself
agreeing with Selye, in part because a
grateful appreciation for pain's
many benefits has so
transformed my
own outlook.

People who view
pain as the enemy,
I have noted, instinctively
respond with vengeance or bitterness—
Why me? I don't deserve this! It's not fair!—
which has the vicious-circle effect of making
their pain even worse. "Think of pain as a speech
your body is delivering about a subject of vital
importance to you," I tell my patients. "From
the very first twinge, pause and listen to the pain
and, yes, try to be grateful. The body is using
the language of pain because that's the most
effective way to get your attention." I call this
approach "befriending" pain: to take what is
ordinarily seen as an enemy and to disarm and
then welcome it.

Give thanks in all circumstances, for this is God's will for you in Christ Jesus.

1 Thessalonians 5:18

How **happy** a person is depends upon the depth of his gratitude.

John Miller

So I give thanks,
Creator Lord,
for pain I once despised.
I've learned to listen, gratefully,
most times my body speaks to me.
It speaks in phrases you prepared, inscribed
   in DNA,
and follows rules that make for health if only
   I obey.
While I rejoice at all the good my senses do
   for me,
I pray for those whose pain defense has
   broken under stress.
When injury or creeping ills yield pain beyond
   control,
then, Lord, reach out your loving hands,
scarred with pain you suffered willingly.
Lift them now and bear them up in fellowship
   with thee.
Though mortal flesh may be in strife,
your peace may fill their conscious life,
from suffering set free.

Dr. Paul Brand

The path to health, for an individual or a society, must begin by taking pain into account. Instead, we silence pain when we should be straining our ears to hear it; we eat too fast and too much and take a seltzer; we work too long and too hard and take a tranquilizer. The three best-selling drugs in the United States are a hypertension drug, a medication for ulcers, and a tranquilizer. These pain-mufflers are readily available because even the medical profession seems to look upon pain as the illness rather than the symptom.

Before heading for the medicine cabinet to silence pain, I try to sharpen my hearing. Listening to pain has become a ritual for me, the flip side of my litany of gratitude. *Is there a pattern to the pain?* I ask myself.

*Does it tend to occur at a regular time of day
or night or month? Does it seem to relate
to my job, or to relationships with people?
How does eating affect it? Do I feel the pain
before, during, or after meals? Does a change
in posture, or abnormal exertion, seem to
affect it? Am I anxious about something in
the future, or do I tend to dwell on some
memory of a past event?* I take notes of any
correlations that come to mind.

I rarely feel grateful for the fact of pain, but
I almost always feel grateful for the message
that it brings. I can count on pain to represent
my best interests in the most urgent way
available. It is then up to me to act on those
recommendations.

During the Middle Ages—a time of chaos and great suffering—religious orders devised a series of contemplative exercises. Most of them included prayer, meditation, and fasting, all disciplines directed toward the inner life. Although intended primarily as worship aids, these disciplines have the added benefit of teaching self-mastery, a form of "pain insurance" that pays good dividends in times of crisis. Meditation (an act of the mind) triggers physiological changes in the body: a gradual lowering of the heart and respiratory rates, changes in brain wave patterns, a general decrease in sympathetic nervous system activity. Tense muscles relax, and a state of inner stress gives way to calmness. In one study, the majority of patients who had failed to find relief for chronic pain in conventional ways reported at least a 50 percent reduction in their pain after training in the relaxation response; in another, three-fourths of the patients reported moderate to great improvement. For this reason, most chronic pain centers now include programs of relaxation and meditation.

I have found that disciplines of the spirit can have an extraordinary effect on the body, and especially on pain. Prayer helps me cope with pain, by moving my mental focus away from a fixation on my body's complaints. As I pray, nourishing the life of the spirit, my tension level goes down and my consciousness of pain tends to recede. It did not surprise me at all to learn recently from a medical researcher that people who have strong religious faith have a lower incident of heart attack, arteriosclerosis, high blood pressure, and hypertension than those who do not.

When one is
in very great pain
and fear, it is extremely
difficult to pray coherently, and I
could only raise my mind in anguish to
God and ask for **strength** to hold on.

Sheila Cassidy

In prayer it is better to have a **heart**
without words, than words without a
heart.

John Bunyan

God insists that we ask, not because
He needs to know our situation,
but because we need the spiritual
discipline of asking.

Catherine Marshall

The Spirit helps us in our weakness.
We do not know what we ought
to pray for, but the Spirit himself
intercedes for us with groans that
words cannot express.

Romans 8:26

Give ear to my words, O Lord,
consider my sighing.
Listen to my cry for help,
my King and my God,
for to you I pray.
In the morning, O Lord, you hear my
voice;
in the morning I lay my requests
before you
and wait in expectation.

Psalm 5:1–3

the importance of community

The best single thing I can do to prepare for
pain is to surround myself with a loving community
who will stand beside me when tragedy strikes. I tend
to rely on my own family as a support community
for pain. A support group can become a community
of shared pain. So can a church or synagogue. My
wife, Margaret, and I may need help in coping with
some emergencies, and we know we can count on
the church community to help shoulder the burden.
Wherever we have lived, we have sought out and
have had the good fortune of finding a caring church.
In fact, our present church has taken the farsighted
step of initiating a home hospice plan. Thirty-two
volunteers have taken a course of training offered by a
local hospital-based program. As long as we are able,
we will each help the others. When we have needs,
they will help us.

The home hospice program relieves some of our anxiety in preparing for death. We have also worked out and signed a "living will" that sets strict limits on the artificial prolonging of life. Death is the one sure fact of life, of course. I trust the words of the psalmist, "Yea, though I walk through the valley of the shadow of death, I will fear no evil, for You are with me." I have learned the best way to disarm my fears about terminal illness, and about the possibility of great pain, is to face them in advance, before God, and within a community that will share them.

Though we do not have our Lord with us in bodily presence, we have our neighbor, who, for the ends of love and **loving service**, is as good as our Lord himself.

St. Teresa of Avila

The LORD is my shepherd, I shall not be in want.
  He makes me lie down in green pastures,
he leads me beside quiet waters,
  he restores my soul.
He guides me in paths of righteousness
  for his name's sake.
Even though I walk
  through the valley of the shadow of death,
I will fear no evil,
  for you are with me;
your rod and your staff,
  they comfort me.
You prepare a table before me
  in the presence of my enemies.
You anoint my head with oil;
  my cup overflows.
Surely goodness and love will follow me
  all the days of my life,
and I will dwell in the house of the LORD
  forever.

Psalm 23

To a very large extent, the course
of healing in any individual patient
depends on what takes place in the
mind. The challenge of medicine is
to find a way to harness the awesome
powers of the mind in

recovery.

Dr. Paul Brand

No matter how well we prepare, pain almost always comes as a surprise. I bend over to pick up a pencil and suddenly it feels as if a spike has been driven into my back. Instantly my concern changes from pain preparation to pain management—and the difference between the two is the difference between a San Francisco practice drill and an actual earthquake. No amount of planning can fully equip us for the time when, without warning, the ground shifts.

I have expressed my suspicion that, in Western countries at least, people have grown increasingly less competent at handling pain and suffering. When pain's emergency sirens sound, the average person trusts his or her own resources less and the "experts" more. I believe the most important step in pain management is to reverse that process. We in medicine need to restore our patients' confidence in the most powerful healer in the world: the human body.

Medicine has
become so complex
and elitist that patients
feel helpless and doubt whether
they have much contribution to make
in the struggle against pain and suffering.
Too often the patient sees himself or herself as a
victim, a sacrificial lamb for the experts to pick
over, not a partner in recovery and health.

On the surface, a doctor's task may resemble
an engineer's—they both repair mechanical
parts—but only on the surface. We treat a person,
not a collection of parts, and a person is far
more than a broken body in need of repair. A
human being, unlike any machine, contains what
Albert Schweitzer called "the doctor within," the
ability to repair itself and to consciously affect
the healing process. The best physicians are the
humblest ones, those who listen closely to the
body and work to assist it in what it is already
instinctively doing for itself. Indeed, in pain
management I have no choice but to work in
partnership: pain occurs "inside" the patient, and
the patient alone can guide me.

The treatment is really a **cooperative effort** of a trinity—the patient, the doctor, and the "inner doctor."

Ralph Bircher

I don't pray that you may be delivered from your troubles. Instead, I pray that God will give you the strength and patience to bear them.

Brother Lawrence

*Praise the LORD, O my soul,
        and forget not all his
benefits—
        who forgives all your sins
                and heals all your
                diseases.*

Psalm 103:2–3

creating conscious distractions

A few years ago I had a problem with my gallbladder. When I first felt the urgent pain signals (stage one) from my upper abdomen, I had no idea to what danger they were trying to alert me. It was an intense and cramping pain, far too severe for indigestion. My age was about right for cancer to appear and, by the time I visited the doctor, I had worked myself into a churning state of fear and foreboding.

An X-ray revealed that I had gallstones, not cancer, a painful condition to be sure, but one easily treatable with surgery. The abdominal attacks kept occurring, but right away they seemed less painful. Although the pain signals themselves did not diminish, my perception of them (stage three) surely changed as my anxiety lessened.

Because of scheduling difficulties, I had to delay the gallbladder surgery for a few months. Pain from gallstones and kidney stones ranks very high on the intensity charts, and I now understand why. I had many opportunities to practice my mastery over pain.

Night attacks were the worst. I remember one especially difficult night when I got out of bed, slipped on a robe, and walked around the paths of the leprosarium in my bare feet. I deliberately chose to walk on the paths made of shell gravel dredged from southern beaches. These shells are very sharp, and painful to bare feet. I had to select my steps with care and ease my feet down gingerly, and I alternated by walking on the wet grass. As I walked along, I also picked up small tree limbs and stones and fingered them. All these minor acts helped to combat the pain: the flood of sensations from the shells on my bare feet competed with and partially drowned out the pain signals from my gallbladder. The pain I felt then was quite different—and much more tolerable—than what I had felt in a dark, quiet bedroom.

The head of medical service in a great university hospital once said, "One should send for his minister (or priest or rabbi) as he sends for his doctor when he becomes ill." That is to say, God **helps** the sick in two ways, through the science of medicine and surgery and through the science of **faith and prayer.**

Norman Vincent Peale

Researchers have unlocked some of the secrets of the brain's alchemy. It seems the body manufactures its own narcotics, which it can release upon command to block out pain. The brain is a master pharmacologist. To stimulate the brain's own painkillers has nearly unlimited potential. Inside the ivory box of skull, psychology and physiology come together. We know that a person's response to pain depends to a very large degree on "subjective" factors, such as emotional preparedness and cultural expectations, which in turn affect the brain's chemistry. By altering these subjective factors, we can directly influence the perception of pain.

For example, the Lamaze course for preparation for childbirth employs one simple exercise that any of us can do at any time to modify pain at stage three: conscious distraction. I first learned of the effect of distraction from Tommy Lewis's research. When bells were rung and adventure stories read aloud, the laboratory volunteers had much greater tolerance for pain. Lab assistants using radiant heat machines were surprised to see blisters swell up unnoticed on volunteers' arms as those subjects concentrated on counting backward from fifty to one.

A few years ago, American dentists had high hopes about the potential of audio techniques in controlling pain. Patients who wore earphones and listened to loud stereo music, or even artificial "white noise," sat contentedly without painkillers while dentists probed and drilled. As long as the subjects concentrated on the music or noise and as long as they had knobs and levers to operate, they felt less pain. They were attending to something else.

Not everyone can master the skill of autosuggestion over pain. But we should be encouraged enough to believe that, even if we cannot abolish a specific pain, we can probably make it hurt less and thus eliminate the need for drugs. All of us carry around atop our necks the amazing capacity for pain management.

Occupy your minds with **good** thoughts,
or the enemy will fill them with bad ones;
unoccupied they cannot be.

Sir Thomas More

Whatever is true, whatever is noble,
whatever is right, whatever is pure,
whatever is lovely, whatever is admirable—
if anything is excellent or praiseworthy—
think about such things.

Philippians 4:8

Why are you downcast, O my soul?
    Why so disturbed within me?
Put your hope in God,
    for I will yet praise him,
    my Savior and my God.

Psalm 43:5

Answer me when I call to you,
*   O my righteous God.*
Give me relief from my distress;
*   be merciful to me and hear my prayer.*
Know that the LORD has set apart the godly
*   for himself;*
*   the LORD will hear when I call to him.*
Many are asking, "Who can show us any
*   good?"*
*   Let the light of your face shine upon*
*   us, O LORD.*
You have filled my heart with greater joy
*   than when their grain and new wine*
*   abound.*
I will lie down and sleep in peace,
*   for you alone, O LORD,*
*   make me dwell in safety.*

*   Psalm 4:1, 3, 6–8*

In the book *Living with Pain,* Barbara Wolf tells of her long struggle against chronic pain, an odyssey which included having subcutaneous neural transmitters implanted in both hands. After trying a host of methods, she decided that distraction was the best and cheapest weapon available. She used to cancel activities when she felt pain, until she noticed that the only time she felt completely free of pain was during classroom hours when she taught English. Wolf recommends work, reading, humor, hobbies, pets, sports, volunteer work, or anything else that can divert the sufferer's mind from pain. When pain strikes with fury in the middle of the night, Wolf gets up, maps out the day ahead, works on a lecture, or completely plans a dinner party.

Pain need not necessarily dull the mind. Blaise Pascal, plagued with acute facial neuralgia, worked out some of his most complex geometry problems while tossing uncomfortably in bed. Composer Robert Schumann, suffering from a chronic illness,

would get out of
bed and correct his
musical scores. Immanuel
Kant, his toes burning from gout,
would concentrate with all his might on
one object—for example, on the Roman orator
Cicero and everything that might relate to him.
Kant claimed this technique succeeded so well
that in the morning he sometimes wondered
whether he had imagined the pain.

One specialist at a chronic pain center told me
that many patients want to wait until the pain
subsides before they resume normal functioning.
But he has learned that coping with chronic pain
depends on a patient's willingness to exercise and
increase productive activity *despite* the feeling of
pain.

Chronic pain management **succeeds**
when the patient accepts the possibility of
living a **useful** life in the presence of pain.

Dr. Paul Brand

Though **perseverance** does not come from
our power, yet it comes within our power.

St. Francis de Sales

I have learned to be content whatever the circumstances. I know what it is to be in need, and I know what it is to have plenty. I have learned the secret of being content in any and every situation, whether well fed or hungry, whether living in plenty or in want. I can do everything through him who gives me strength.

Philippians 4:11–13

It is God who works in you to will and to act according to his good purpose.

Philippians 2:13

Therefore we do not lose heart. Though outwardly we are wasting away, yet inwardly we are being renewed day by day. For our light and momentary troubles are achieving for us an eternal glory that far outweighs them all. So we fix our eyes not on what is seen, but on what is unseen. For what is seen is temporary, but what is unseen is eternal.

2 Corinthians 4:16–18

Transcutaneous stimulators, epidural blocks, spinal cordotomies—these techniques may help persistent, long-term pain, but in many cases the body finds a new avenue and the pain returns. For this reason, chronic pain centers have learned to attack pain on all three fronts: signals from the injury site, messages along the transmission routes, and responses in the mind. Actually, attending to a patient's psychological health and family environment may have as much effect on the pain as prescribing analgesic drugs or a Transcutaneous Electrical Nerve Stimulator (TENS) device.

In my own approach to pain, I give highest priority to the third stage (the brain). That may seem odd, since I have spent so much of my career working with leprosy patients, who suffer from the lack of pain signals in the periphery (stage one). But the very fact that they do "suffer" proves the importance of the mind in the pain experience. Leprosy patients helped me understand the difference between *pain* and *suffering.* "I'm suffering in my mind because I can't suffer in my body" is how my patient Namo put it.

In more advanced cases of leprosy, my patients felt no "pain" at all: no negative sensations reached their brains when they touched a hot stove or stepped on a nail. Yet all of them suffered, as greatly as any people I have ever known. They lost the freedom that pain provides, they lost the sense of touch and sometimes sight, they lost their physical attractiveness, and, because of the stigma of the disease, they lost the feeling of acceptance by fellow human beings. The mind responded to these effects of painlessness with a feeling that could only be called suffering.

For the rest of us, pain and suffering often arrive in the same package. My goal in pain management is to seek ways to employ the human mind as an ally, not an adversary. In other words, can I prevent "pain" from becoming undue "suffering"? The mind offers wonderful resources to accomplish just that.

I consider that our present sufferings are not worth comparing with the glory that will be revealed in us.

Romans 8:18

Jesus did not come to explain away suffering or remove it. He came to fill it with His Presence.

Paul Claudel

The only **cure** for suffering is to face it head on, grasp it 'round the neck, and use it.

Mary Craig

May your unfailing love come to me, O Lord,
your salvation according to your
promise.
Remember your word to your servant,
for you have given me hope.
My comfort in my suffering is this:
Your promise preserves my life.
Your word is a lamp to my feet
and a light for my path.
I have taken an oath and confirmed it,
that I will follow your righteous laws.
I have suffered much;
preserve my life, O Lord, according to
your word.
Accept, O Lord, the willing praise of my
mouth,
and teach me your laws.
Look upon my suffering and deliver me,
for I have not forgotten your law.
Defend my cause and redeem me;
preserve my life according to your
promise.
May my cry come before you, O Lord;
give me understanding according to
your word.

Psalm 119:41,49–50,105–
108,153–154,169

overcoming the intensifiers of pain

I use the term "pain intensifiers" for responses that heighten the perception of pain within the conscious mind. These intensifiers— fear, anger, guilt, loneliness, helplessness—may have more impact on the overall *experience* of pain than any prescription drug you might take.

Dr. Paul Brand

Fear is the **strongest** intensifier of pain.

Dr. Paul Brand

In measurable physiological ways, fear increases pain. When an injured person is afraid, muscles tense and contract, increasing the pressure on damaged nerves and causing even more pain. Blood pressure and vasodilation change, too, which is why a frightened person goes pale or flushes red. Sometimes this product of the mind translates into actual bodily damage, as is the case with spastic colon, a by-product of human anxiety unknown in other animal species.

I encourage patients to talk about their fear so that together we can relate the fear to the pain signal. Fear, like pain, can be good or bad. Good fear backs me away from cliffs and makes me duck when I hear a loud noise. It stops me from taking foolish risks when I drive a car or go downhill skiing. Problems only develop when fear (or pain) grows out of proportion to the danger.

A friend of mine in California, Tim Hansel, taught me an important lesson about good fear and bad fear. An enthusiastic outdoorsman, Tim directed a program that led strenuous camping trips to the Sierra Nevada Mountains. On one of these trips, he fell headfirst into a crevasse, striking a rock at the bottom. The impact compressed his spinal vertebrae together, rupturing discs in his upper back, and soon arthritis settled in the bones. Hansel lived with constant, intense pain. He consulted several specialists, and each one told him the same thing: "You'll just have to live with the pain. Surgery can't help."

As the months stretched into years, Hansel learned various ways to cope with the pain. Afraid of causing further injury, he cut back on many of his activities. In time, however, his spirits sank. The sedentary life was making him depressed. Finally, Hansel voiced his fears to his doctor. "I've been afraid of reinjuring myself, but it's driving me crazy. I feel paralyzed by the fear. Tell me specifically, what must I avoid? What might cause more damage?"

His doctor thought for a moment and replied, "The damage is irreversible. I suppose I would recommend against painting eaves—that would put too great a strain on your neck. But as far as I can tell, you can do whatever else the pain will allow you to do." According to Hansel, that word from the doctor gave him a new lease on life. For the first time, he realized that he was in control of his pain, his future, his life. He determined to live the only way he knew—with a sense of abandonment. He went back to climbing mountains and leading expeditions.

Tim Hansel's pain did not go away. But his fear did. And Hansel found that with the reduction in fear, his pain eventually decreased as well. I have been with Tim and believe him when he says that pain no longer has any negative effect on the quality of his life. He has learned to master it, because he no longer fears it. "My pain is unavoidable," he says. "But my misery is optional."

Be strong and courageous. Do not be terrified; do not be discouraged, for the LORD your God will be with you wherever you go.

Joshua 1:9

The LORD is my light and my salvation—
  whom shall I fear?
The LORD is the stronghold of my life—
  of whom shall I be afraid?

Psalm 27:1

I am in pain and distress;
  may your salvation, O God, protect me.

Psalm 69:29

I lift up my eyes to the hills—
*   where does my help come from?*
My help comes from the Lord,
*   the Maker of heaven and earth.*

He will not let your foot slip—
*   he who watches over you will not*
*   slumber;*
indeed, he who watches over Israel
*   will neither slumber nor sleep.*

The Lord watches over you—
*   the Lord is your shade at your right*
*   hand;*
the sun will not harm you by day,
*   nor the moon by night.*

The Lord will keep you from all harm—
*   he will watch over your life;*
the Lord will watch over your coming and
*   going*
*   both now and forevermore.*

Psalm 121

To hate is easy, but it is healthier to **love.**

Bernie Siegel

Hand surgeons dread one condition above all others: "reflex sympathetic dystrophy" (RSD), a particular manifestation of the stiff hand phenomenon. After an injury or minor surgical procedure, severe pain may begin to spread throughout a limb. Muscles go into periodic spasm. The hand swells and the skin tightens. Inexplicably, over time the hand locks up and becomes as stiff as a mannequin's.

Sheer anger provoked the most dramatic case of stiff hand I have seen. In India, I treated a patient who had lost the tip of her nose. She had a beautiful face, even with the thickened skin around her surgically repaired nose, but as she told me the story of the stiff hand, her face contorted in rage—curiously, against the surgeon who repaired the nose and not the husband who bit it off.

She had gone to a plastic surgeon in Madras, who agreed to fashion a new tip for her nose out of abdominal skin. First he cut a strip of skin from the abdomen, leaving it attached to the belly at one end and lifting the other end free to form a bridge to the side of her wrist. In order to allow the graft time to develop a new blood supply in the wrist, he kept her hand strapped to the abdomen for three weeks.

Afterward, in a second operation, the surgeon snipped the bridge at the belly end so that the strip of skin hung free. He lifted Lakshmi's hand to her forehead, letting the tube of skin hang in front of her nose. His plan was to come back at the end of three weeks and cut the hand free of the tube of skin, leaving a new tip of nose on the base of the old.

Lakshmi awoke from surgery feeling pain in her shoulder. The surgeon, probably assuming that a young woman would have a perfectly free joint, had never bothered to find out that she had suffered from arthritis in her shoulder for some years and had never been able to lift her arm freely without pain. Now she found her arm strapped into a position that caused constant pain. Day after day she screamed at the doctor, telling him she couldn't bear the pain in her shoulder. He made light of the problem.

By the time the surgeon removed the strapping around her head and finished the nose, Lakshmi had an advanced case of reflex sympathetic dystrophy. Her entire arm, from shoulder to hand, was hypersensitive to pain, and the hand absolutely was immobile. Whenever she tried to move her hand, the muscles went into a kind of spasm and the fingers refused to bend.

On the operating table, with Lakshmi under anesthesia, I could bend the fingers to some extent. I performed a second surgery on the hand, and my therapists tried to restore motion by splinting and massage. But the hand behaved as though it was determined to be stiff. Each time, the muscle spasms returned. I concluded the woman had lost the use of her hand because of anger and distress. I could find no other physiological cause.

Physiologically, we do not really understand why a hand may become stiff after a minor injury, but we do know that it is more likely to happen when anger and bitterness are present. Lakshmi in India may have been the most dramatic case of RSD I have witnessed, but I must say there are more cases proportionately in the United States. I have since concluded that the litigiousness in the United States provides much more fertile ground for anger, resentment, and frustration, the very feelings that foster conditions like reflex sympathetic dystrophy.

Too often I have seen the physiological effect on people who became angry with their employer, or the driver of the other car, or the previous surgeon, or a spouse who lacked sympathy, or God. The anger must be dealt with, of course; it does not go away on its own. But if it is not dealt with, if it is allowed to fester in the mind and soul, the anger may release its poison in the body, affecting pain and healing.

Our anger and annoyance are more detrimental to us than the things themselves which anger or annoy us.

Marcus Aurelius

A gentle answer turns away wrath, but a harsh word stirs up anger.

Proverbs 15:1

Refrain from anger and turn from wrath;
do not fret—it leads only to evil.

Psalm 37:8

Do not let the sun go down while you
are still angry.

Ephesians 4:26

You must rid yourselves of all such
things as these: anger, rage, malice,
slander, and filthy language from
your lips.

Colossians 3:8

I cannot point precisely to a tangible proof of guilt's effect on pain. But after a career spent among leprosy patients, who are made to feel uniquely cursed by God, I know well that guilt compounds mental suffering. Counselors at chronic pain centers, too, report that their most challenging, "pain-prone" patients have deep-rooted feelings of guilt and may well interpret their pain as a form of punishment.

Dr. Paul Brand

When I was a child living in London, the elderly vicar of a neighborhood church slipped on a banana peel and fell on the sidewalk. We children joked about it: *Imagine, he fell on the way to church! A banana peel! Maybe he had his eyes closed, praying.* But then we learned he had broken his hip in the fall, and we stopped laughing. Weeks rolled by, and the vicar was not released from the hospital. Infection set in, then pneumonia, and finally the vicar died. We felt ashamed of our laughter.

That experience stayed with me as I later tried to sort through the issues of guilt and punishment. Who was at fault? Obviously not the banana peel itself, which was perfectly designed to keep a banana fresh and clean until it is eaten or drops to seed a new tree. And the incident could hardly be called an "act of God." God had not placed the banana peel on the pavement; it was left there by some thoughtless person who did not care about clean sidewalks or hazards to elderly people. Even at a young age, I reasoned that though there had been a human agent, the litterer, the banana-peel accident was just that, an accident, and implied no hidden message from God.

I cannot always determine scientifically what has caused a given disease. And I cannot always answer "Why?" questions for my patients. Sometimes I ask them myself. But whenever I can, and whenever my patients seem open, I do my best to relieve them of oppressive, unnecessary guilt.

When my father
died, my aunts quoted
the text from Romans 8:28:
"All things work together for good to
them that love God." I felt relieved later on
when I learned that the Greek original text is
more properly translated, "In everything that
happens, God works for good with those who
love him." I have found that promise to hold true
in all the disasters and hardships I have known
personally. Things happen, some of them good,
some of them bad, many of them beyond our
control. In all these things, I have felt the reliable
constant of God's willingness to work with me
and through me to produce some good.

Cast all your anxiety on him because he cares for you.

1 Peter 5:7

The LORD is compassionate and gracious,
  slow to anger, abounding in love.
He will not always accuse,
  nor will he harbor his anger forever;
he does not treat us as our sins deserve
  or repay us according to our iniquities.
For as high as the heavens are above the earth,
  so great is his love for those who fear him;
as far as the east is from the west,
  so far has he removed our transgressions
    from us.

Psalm 103:8–12

The presence of a **caring** person can have an actual, measurable effect on pain and on healing.

Dr. Paul Brand

Loneliness comes in the same package with pain since pain, perceived in the mind, belongs uniquely to me and cannot truly be shared. Yet, though no one else can perceive my physical pain, there is another, deeper sense in which pain can indeed be shared.

Early in my career I heard a lecture from the anthropologist Margaret Mead. "What would you say is the earliest sign of civilization?" she asked, naming a few options. A clay pot? Tools made of iron? The first domesticated plants? "These are all early signs," she continued, "but here is what I believe to be evidence of the earliest true civilization." High above her head she held a human femur, the largest bone in the leg, and pointed to a grossly thickened area where the bone had been fractured, and then solidly healed. "Such signs of healing are never found among the remains of the earliest, fiercest societies. In their skeletons we find clues of violence: a rib pierced by an arrow, a skull crushed by a club. But this healed bone shows that someone must have cared for the injured

person—
hunted on his
behalf, brought him food,
served him at personal sacrifice."
With Margaret Mead, I believe that this
quality of shared pain is central to what it means
to be a human being.

Ministering to the loneliness of a suffering person requires no professional expertise. When I have asked, "Who helped you most?" usually patients describe a quiet, unassuming person: someone who was there whenever needed, who listened more than talked, who didn't keep glancing down at a watch, who hugged and touched and cried. One woman, a cancer patient, mentioned her grandmother, a rather shy lady who had nothing to offer but time. She simply sat in a chair and knitted while her granddaughter slept, and made herself available to talk, or fetch a glass of water, or make a phone call. "She was the only person there on my terms," said the granddaughter. "When I woke up frightened, it would reassure me just to see her there."

Over the years I have learned that we in the health profession have more to offer than drugs and bandages. Standing side-by-side with patients and families in their suffering is a form of treatment in itself.

It is the experience of touching the pain of others that is the key to change....Compassion is a sign of transformation.

Jim Wallis

God is absent from the world, except in the existence in this world of those in whom his love is alive. Therefore they ought to be in the world through •

compassion.

Their compassion is the visible presence of God here below.

Simone Weil

I will praise the LORD, who
counsels me;
even at night my heart instructs me.
I have set the LORD always before me.
Because he is at my right hand,
I will not be shaken.
Therefore my heart is glad and my
tongue rejoices;
my body also will rest secure,
because you will not abandon me to
the grave,
nor will you let your Holy One see decay.
You have made known to me the path of life;
you will fill me with joy in your presence,
with eternal pleasures at your right hand.

Psalm 16:7–11

By helping yourself, you are helping mankind.
By helping mankind, you are helping yourself.
That's the law of all spiritual **progress.**

Christopher Isherwood

When I was in medical residency during World
War II, I saw proof of the positive benefits that
can result when patients feel useful. Britain
was suffering heavy casualties on the European
front, and the military ordered a sudden call-up
of nurses. Our hospital staff decimated, we had
no choice but to ask patients to fill in. Patriotic
feeling was running high, and most patients
eagerly volunteered.

The nursing supervisor, a lively woman who
would have made a fine drill instructor, assigned
duties to every patient who could walk, and even
a few in wheelchairs. They fetched bedpans,
changed sheets, distributed food and water, and
took temperature and blood pressure readings.
The few remaining nurses concentrated on
dealing with prescription drugs and IVs, and
keeping records. The system worked well, and it
produced one rather extraordinary side benefit:
patients got so caught up in caring for each
other's suffering that they forgot

about their own. I noticed a nearly 50 percent drop in demands for pain medication. On my night rounds, I found that patients who usually needed sleeping pills were peacefully asleep by the time I came around. After a few weeks of this emergency program, the hospital recruited more nurses and relieved the patients of their volunteer duties. Dosages almost immediately went back up, and the usual atmosphere of helplessness and lethargy wafted in.

Some chronic-pain clinics battle helplessness by negotiating "contracts" with their patients. First the staff encourages the patient to articulate a long-term goal: to play tennis, to walk a mile, to get a part-time job. Then, working as a team, they break the goal into smaller, weekly goals: holding a tennis racket, walking across the room with a cane, and then walking without a cane. Medical personnel chart the patient's weekly progress and praise each new step, thereby shifting the emphasis from helplessness to achievement. Friends and relatives can accomplish the very same thing by forming a "contract" with the

recovering person,
and then rewarding any
slight victory over helplessness.
Far too often, however, well-intentioned
helpers do just the opposite. I find when I am
sick that everyone conspires to keep me from
doing anything—"It's for your own good, of
course," they say.

Suffering people, like all of us, want to cling
to some assurance that they have a place, that
life would not go on without a bump if they
simply disappeared, that the checkbook would
go unbalanced except for their expert attention.
Wise helpers learn to seek out the delicate
balance between offering help and offering too
much help.

Jesus said, "I tell you the truth, whatever you
did for one of the least of these brothers of
mine, you did for me."

Matthew 25:40

One of the most important gifts we in the health profession can offer our patients is

hope,

thereby inspiring in the patient a deep conviction that inner strength can make a difference in the struggle against pain and suffering.

Dr. Paul Brand

In the field of rehabilitation, my primary challenge has been to get my patients to accept that they alone can determine their fate. I can repair a hand; whether it works again is up to them. I have not completed my job unless I somehow inspire them to seek health so that they deeply *want* to get well. I have been blessed to know many exceptional patients over the years, leprosy patients who overcame incredible odds to find a rich and fulfilling life for themselves.

One of the most "exceptional patients" I ever met, though, was Norman Cousins himself. I mainly remember Cousins's bright, active mind. He had boundless curiosity and seemed fascinated by every obscure detail of our research into pain.

The story of Norman Cousins's personal battle against suffering is well-known. He adopted a personal program of fighting back against "pain intensifiers," a program that has inspired patients around the world. For example, he battled the feeling of helplessness by posting a sign on his door limiting hospital personnel to one blood specimen every three days, which they had to share. He fought anger by borrowing a movie projector and watching movies by comedians like the Marx Brothers and Charlie Chaplin. He made the "joyous discovery that ten minutes of genuine belly laughter would give me at least two hours of painfree sleep."

Cousins's entire approach was based on his belief that, since negative emotions demonstrably produce chemical changes in the body, then positive emotions—hope, faith, love, joy, the will to live, creativity, playfulness—should counteract them and help drive out the intensifiers of pain. In his last years, Cousins moved to the UCLA medical school and founded a research group to study the effect of positive attitudes on health.

Cousins conducted a survey of 649 oncologists, asking them what psychological and emotional factors in their patients they judged important. More than 90 percent replied that they attached the highest value to attitudes of hope and optimism.

Near the end of his life, Norman Cousins wrote, "Nothing I have learned in the past decade at the medical school seems to me more striking than the need of patients for reassurance. . . . Illness is a terrifying experience. Something is happening that people don't know how to deal with. They are reaching out not just for medical help but for ways of thinking about catastrophic illness. They are reaching out for hope."

It is only when everything is hopeless that hope begins to be a

strength

at all.
G. K. Chestertor

With God all things are possible.

Matthew 19:26

Jesus said, "I have told you these things, so that in me you may have peace. In this world you will have trouble. But take heart! I have overcome the world."

John 16:33

Find rest, O my soul, in God alone;
  my hope comes from him.
He alone is my rock and my salvation;
  he is my fortress, I will not be shaken.
My salvation and my honor depend
    on God;
  he is my mighty rock, my refuge.
Trust in him at all times, O people;
  pour out your hearts to him,
  for God is our refuge.

Psalm 62:5–8

I once met with nuns, caregivers, and a few pain specialists from around the world at a conference in Dallas, Texas. In a televised interview afterward, I explained my personal philosophy of pain based on gratitude and appreciation for pain's benefits. "The system of pain is good," I said, "even though there will surely be times when individual pains are not good." I mentioned the pain that sometimes accompanies terminal cancer, a debilitating pain that serves no helpful purpose—the patient knows death is coming soon—and frustrates most pain-management techniques.

"The challenge of medicine in such a case," I said, "is to give enough medication to quell the pain, but not so much as to cloud the patient's mind. Yet if the pain persists, as an act of mercy it may be necessary to give so much medication that the patient may not be conscious enough to communicate."

I heard a sudden eruption at the other end of the table and turned to face a slim, distinguished-looking Englishwoman. Dr. Therese Vanier had almost jumped out of her seat. "I'm sorry, Dr. Brand, but I must strongly disagree! I am a physician at the St. Christopher's Hospice in London, and this is not the philosophy of our hospice! We promise our patients that they will be free of severe pain but also will remain lucid. We can almost guarantee that."

The vigor of Dr. Vanier's response startled me, and after the interview I sought her out. She invited me to visit the hospice founded by Dame Cicely Saunders in 1967, in order to observe what they had learned about worst-case, terminal pain.

"The majority of patients come to us in severe pain, in the final stages of their illness," Vanier explained during my visit. "Pain from a terminal disease is unique. Pain from a bone fracture, sore tooth, childbirth, or even postoperative recovery has meaning, and there is an end in sight. Pain from progressive cancer has no meaning except the constant reminder of approaching death. For many of the patients who come to us, pain fills the entire horizon. They can't eat, sleep, pray, think, or relate to people without being dominated by pain. Here at St. Christopher's, we try to combat that particular kind of pain."

After visiting with Vanier, I met with Dr. Cicely Saunders, who told me the origin of the hospice movement. She had founded the first hospice, she said, after seeing how poorly the medical profession handled death. For the sake of a patient with some prospect of recovery, a modern hospital would go to any length. But a patient without hope was an embarrassment, a shameful emblem of medicine's failures. Doctors mostly avoided terminally ill patients, or spoke to them in platitudes and half-truths. Treatment for their pain tended to be grossly inadequate. In the midst of busy, crowded hospitals, terminal patients died afraid and very much alone.

The standard treatment of terminal patients offended Saunder's deep Christian sensibilities. A nurse at the time, she enrolled in medical school at the age of thirty-three for the express purpose of finding a better way to minister to the dying. She founded St. Christopher's, and out of that sprang the worldwide hospice movement.

Working together, Saunders and Vanier pioneered the "preventive" approach to pain from terminal disease. Saunders carefully determined dosages in advance, then made them available to the patient at regular intervals so that the pain never returned at all. A steady blood level of medication, she found, helps to prevent both severe pain and oversedation. Under supervision, they usually come up with a program that controls pain around the clock without mental clouding.

My day at St. Christopher's convinced me that Therese Vanier's outburst on the panel in Dallas was fully justified. Even the worst pain imaginable, the severe pain that accompanies terminal illness, need not debilitate. It struck me that Dame Cicely, Dr. Vanier, and the others at St. Christopher's have incorporated nearly everything I have learned about pain management and more. They allow for diversion and conscious distraction. They help soothe the subjective factors (fear, anxiety) that contribute to pain. They work hard to make the patient feel like a partner, not a victim, one who retains control over his or her own body. They create a caring community.

In a word, the hospice movement has shifted the focus of medicine from *cure* to *care.*

St. Christopher's, which grew out of one woman's deep Christian compassion, shows what can be done. Many church and community groups have followed Dame Cicely's model and now extend loving care to the terminally ill who have chosen against artificial methods of prolonging life.

By definition, these patients are beyond the range of medical cure. Yet hospice has found a way to treat this most distressing human condition with dignity and compassion. Dame Cicely takes pride in the fact that fully 95 percent of the patients at St. Christopher's have been able to stay both alert and free of pain. She has demonstrated it is possible to disarm the last great fear most of us will face, the fear of death and the pain which accompanies it.

Suffering is only intolerable when nobody cares. One continually sees that faith in God and his care is made infinitely easier by faith in someone who has shown kindness and sympathy.

Cicely Saunders

I cannot end a section on pain without raising the issue of God's concern for human suffering. How does God view the suffering of his creatures? Does it affect him?

The Bible gives overwhelming emphasis to God's passionate involvement with creation. It is virtually a catalog of God's emotions in relating to humanity. From creation onward, God places himself in the position of an anxious Father whose children run free. Clearly, events arouse in God either joy or sorrow, pleasure or wrath. The Old Testament portrays a God who is not "wholly other" or remote, but One involved with creation. God goes with his people into exile, into captivity, into the fiery furnace, into the grave.

God voluntarily put himself in the position of being affected by creation. Love involves giving, and God, self-complete, has only himself to give. God surely does not suffer out of some deficiency of being, as his creatures do, but from the love that overflows from being. Imagining pain is one thing—God as designer has surely understood its

physiological
values and
limitations. Grieving
in response to pain, feeling
with his people, suffering with
humanity—all these, too, linked God
and man. Still, something is missing.

Until God took on the soft tissue of flesh along with its pain cells just as accurate and subject to abuse as ours, God had not truly experienced pain. By sending the Son to earth, God learned to feel pain in the same way we feel pain. Our prayer and cries of suffering take on greater meaning because we now know them to be understood by God. Instinctively, we want a God who not only knows about pain, but shares in it and is affected by our own. By looking at Jesus, we realize we have such a God. He took on the limitation of time and space and family and pain and sorrow.

Christ did not, however, stop at identification and shared experience. In the resurrection that followed his death on the cross, he transformed the nature of pain.

He overthrew the powers of this world by first allowing sin to do its worst, then transmuting that act into his best. The most meaningless of all acts, his own innocent death, became the most meaningful.

The apostle Paul explored this change in a hymn at the end of Romans 8. No one can condemn us, he says, because of Christ Jesus who died and was raised to life and now is present with the Father. Now, nothing can separate us from the love of Christ, not the pains of trouble or hardship or persecution or famine or nakedness or danger or sword. No, he concludes, we are all more than conquerors through him who loved us. And then this summing up: "For I am convinced that neither death nor life, neither angels nor demons, neither the present nor the future [time], nor any powers, neither height nor depth [space], nor anything else in all creation, will be able to separate us from the love of God that is in Christ Jesus our Lord."

This, then, is the conclusion of pain. God takes the Great Pain of the Son's death and uses it to blot up into himself all the minor pains of our own confinement on earth. Meaningless pain is absorbed. God absorbs our own pain so that what we endure becomes a part of what he suffered and will become a part of what is resurrected in triumph and transformed into good. God hears and understands our pain, and even absorbs it into himself—because he kept those scars of the crucifixion in his resurrected body as a lasting image of wounded humanity. God has been here and has borne the sentence. The pain of humanity has become the pain of God.

Bodily pain affects man as a whole down to the deepest layers of his moral being. It forces him to face again the fundamental questions of his fate, of his attitude toward God and fellow man, of his individual and collective responsibility and of the sense of his pilgrimage on earth.

Pope Pius XII

"Death has been swallowed up in victory."
    "Where, O death, is your victory?
    Where, O death, is your sting?"
But thanks be to God! He gives us the
victory through our Lord Jesus Christ.

1 Corinthians 15:55, 57

And the God of all grace, who called you
to his eternal glory in Christ, after you
have suffered a little while, will himself
restore you and make you strong, firm and
steadfast. To him be the power for ever
and ever. Amen.

1 Peter 5:10–11

Our citizenship is in heaven. And we
eagerly await a Savior from there, the
Lord Jesus Christ, who, by the power that
enables him to bring everything under his
control, will transform our lowly bodies so
that they will be like his glorious body.

Philippians 3:20–21

Everywhere a **greater joy** is preceded by a greater suffering.

Saint Augustine

This insight into pleasure is one that we in the affluent West need to remember. We dare not allow our daily lives to become so comfortable that we are no longer challenged to grow, to seek adventure, to risk. An internal self-mastery builds when you run farther than you have run before, when you climb a mountain higher than any other, when you take a sauna bath and then roll in the snow. The adventures themselves bring exhilaration; meanwhile, challenge, risk, and pain combine to bolster a confidence that may serve well in times of crises.

In short, if I spend my life seeking pleasure through drugs, comfort, and luxury, it will probably elude me. Lasting pleasure is more apt to come as a surprising bonus from something in which I have invested myself. Most likely that investment will include pain—it is hard to imagine pleasure without it.

I take comfort in the fact that somehow, in the mysterious resources of the human spirit, even pain can serve a **higher end.**

Dr. Paul Brand

Ah, Lord God, thou holy lover of my soul,
when thou comest into my soul, all that is
    within me shall rejoice.
Thou art my glory and the exultation of my
    heart;
thou art my hope and refuge in the day of
    my trouble.
Set me free from all evil passions,
    and heal my heart of all inordinate
        affections;
that being inwardly cured and thoroughly
    cleansed,
I may be made fit to love, courageous to
    suffer, steady to persevere.

amen. *Thomas à Kempis*

sources

Appleton, George. *The Oxford Book of Prayer.* New York, NY: Oxford University Press, 1985.

Bangley, Bernard, comp. *Near to the Heart of God: Daily Reading from the Spiritual Classics.* Wheaton, IL: Harold Shaw Publishers, 1998.

Brand, Dr. Paul and Philip Yancey. *In the Likeness of God.* Grand Rapids, MI: Zondervan, 2004.

Brand, Dr. Paul and Philip Yancey. *Pain: The Gift Nobody Wants.* New York, NY: HarperCollins Publishers, 1993.

At Inspirio, we love to hear from you—your stories, your feedback, and your product ideas. Please send your comments to us by way of email at
icares@zondervan.com
or to the address below:

inspirio

Attn: Inspirio Cares
5300 Patterson Avenue SE
Grand Rapids, MI 49530
If you would like further information about Inspirio and the products we create, please visit us at
www.inspiriogifts.com

Thank you and God bless!